Godmanstone Blues

Godmanstone Blues

Chris Bond

Illustrated by
Andy Paciorek

The Cornovia Press

First published in 2007 by The Cornovia Press

Second Edition (Illustrated, Revised and Enlarged) 2012

Third Edition (Revised and Enlarged) 2020

Text © Chris Bond 1988-2016
Illustrations © Andy Paciorek 2009

All rights reserved. No part of this publication may be reproduced, stored in a retrieval system, or transmitted in any form or by any means, electronic, mechanical, photocopying, recording or otherwise, without the prior permission of the copyright holders.

ISBN 978 1 908878 17 5

*To my dear old friend and ally Sibs
      I dedicate these righteous fibs*

VANADIUM

Please find some logic between thy knees
Else I be forced to unravel thee
Like finest threads of Milano lace
And cast thee into outer space

Please find some substance in thy head
Else I be forced, with mortal dread
To deconstruct thy matter base
And cast thee into outer space

Please find some lyric in thy tongue
Else I be forced, before too long
To pluck off thine offensive face
And cast thee into outer space

Please find some love within thy heart
Else I be forced to wrench apart
Thy agèd soul with God's own grace
And cast thee into outer space

GARGOYLE

I am the gargoyle in the recess of your mind
Sitting, stone shitting, your soul is mine
I'm waiting here...so patiently
Petrified huh...you fucking should be
I am the gargoyle crawling up your arse
Sitting in your colon, sucking in your gas
Boring through your bowels, the pleasure's all mine
Don't take it to heart, this is killing time

I am the gargoyle in the alcove of your brain
In your central nervous system, gonna fill it up with pain
I'm dancing in your ears to the beat of your lies
Got a front row seat for your demise
I am the gargoyle slipping down your throat
Feeding on your essence, I'm the horny goat
Your acid reign gut's just a festering maze
Sifting through the shit of life's vilest ways

I am the gargoyle in the altar of your life
I am your saviour, your ethereal midwife
I am intravenous, your morphine wrap
Just sitting here waiting to spring my trap
I am the gargoyle squatting in your heart
If you give it away I'm gonna tear you apart
I'm waiting here...so patiently
Petrified huh...you fucking should be

Blood, bile, phlegm

Puss, saliva, semen

The building blocks of men

In the dusty heart of Yemen

The Phantoms of a Thousand Years

Oh how they mock these heartfelt dreams

In play upon my wrist

Like dance of knights to represent

The ecstasy I'd kissed

Three fingers rise to strip away

The webs which we conceived

Within our minds when we inclined

To practise to deceive

What irks me though is that these words

Seem now so second hand

And though the hand was also mine

You chose to countermand

Counterpoised twixt now and then

Like logan stone on hill

Where ravens perch and gently rock

The triumph of my will

Sovereignty stirs below my feet

She sings a sweet and bitter air

To tell of Luca's 'deeds' made flesh

To tell of guarded souls laid bare

Oppression, flood and famine

War and wealth and wrath

This bondage you have chosen

Is the dark and downward path

This flesh and blood is mortal stuff

And wont to decompose

To energy from whence it came

And on the story goes

Tie-Dyed and Legless

Another freight train rumbled past, and I took the vibrations and guided them into the pits of my groin, gradually increasing the pressure on my temples with the palms of my hands. The last of the 23 carriages brought me off, and my legs glided down to dead weight, quivering as I opened my eyes. Red digital 3:33 hovered midway up west wall, and I arched the corner of the doss-bag to one side. I dipped the tips of my fingers into the saline pool and slowly massaged the mousse into the metal rash below my navel. My stubborn belief in the antiseptic qualities of sperm warmed the back of my mind, and I pulled the doss-bag back over my head, and melted back into catharsis.

Asleep I found myself in Tucson. I turned to face the stone bridge on all fours, and sank my teeth into the Euclid sidewalk. Five teeth shattered, and the abscess drained into a small pool between my hands. Above me, five F15s headed south-south-east, Colombia way. My ears bled, and I rolled myself down the bank and into the dry wash, silver druid peeking out at me from beneath the sand. The Shadowmass passed me on the right, crossed the wash, and concealed itself behind the rusted pick-up. I sniffed the weeds and fought the urge to urinate. The side of the bank turned to sand as my fingers grasped for mercy. I now saw the white corrugated shack to my right, and I pushed the fibres out through my stomach, and onto the mealy-morsel opuntia squatting by the front door. The grey blind dog saw me and growled, bared it's yellowed teeth and turned it's head to my left, sensed for a few seconds, then turned and ran. I contracted the fibres and felt a face full of spines. I took the keys from my pocket and opened the door, locking it behind me. The Shadowmass landed on the roof causing a dry moan. I reached for the lamp and located the switch. As the light came on I noticed the web on the lampshade and the widow bit.

Outside, the gravel crunched under the weight of a Plymouth. I sat on the swivel chair and extracted a camel, manny, moe & jacked it, and listened to the car door shut. The Plymouth reversed back up the dirt road, the sound fading behind the opaque jelly beginning to coat my senses. I was falling fast as you leaned over me and looked into my lactic eyes. A trace image of your face lingered on in my mind, followed closely by the inside of my skull as I was sucked backwards out of my carcass. I floated for a while, and landed on my back in the soft sands of the eternal Sonoran desert, where the saguaro greeted me with waving arms and smiles that split from side to side. I moved forward rapidly, and wondered why I hadn't always had eight legs. As I started to search for you, the dub pounded and I awoke.

GLEBE LANDS

In crow-sport graveyard can be found

In vaguest shade of oaken glade

Long-cut girls with hasty breasts

All swollen 'neath their stringy vests

But mark thy time by rise and fall

Of their delights, for tomorrow's nigh

When we become the earth subsumed

As flesh turns worm turns blackbird pie

Jack of Arts

I am the Jack of many arts

But in life my main profession

Is to personify the Jack of hearts

When meeting life's digressions

Yezidi

My one and only wish

That you were a Yezidi

I'd encircle you with chalk

And always you'd be with me

QUOS DEUS VULT PERDERE, PRIUS DEMENTAT

Penetrate, then deviate
In quest to circumnavigate
From pole to pole, and back again
The soulless void of man's chagrin
No peace of mind, just endless days
Forever searching Troytown maze
No man can e'er acclimatise
Beneath these ever shifting skies

Weep like willow, shed the tears
To fill this ocean, year by year
No longitude, no night lit stars
No latitudes to warm the scars
No atlas here of lands immense
No turning back, no recompense
"Varium et mutabile
semper femina" I feel

Terra Incognito

Sometimes the angels cast doubt on my ability to flow

Like a mountain stream cascading over basalt cliffs

Which have stood since the dawn of time

They echo tones in long forgotten tongues

Not spoken since the days when this land

And I were both young and unrestrained

In the days before the breath of life began

And when the fiery moon still filled half the sky

She cools and retreats and lengthens the days

Yet still the days seem to pass ever more swiftly

And plans once born in the exuberance of youth

Have grown into monsters

Demanding ever more of my attention

So I find myself in reverie atop the mountains

Where eagles soar across an endless sky

And the streams cascade over basalt cliffs

Which have stood since the dawn of time

EL ESCOGIDO

She held a visionary's stance, like a child who spies a comet for the first time; head thrown back and legs apart, long auburn hair trailing in the wind. She caught a glimpse of it once, but it melted away and was gone. That's nearly always the way it is. She called it the white rush, like God's supernova snowball. She saw it by the Thayer on the bedroom wall. I used to find her searching under floorboards, brambles, park benches, and old copies of the Radio Times; anywhere she might care to find it. She would beam and wander round the flat in her underwear for days on end. She was never happier than when she was searching indoors, and neither was I. She never seemed to lose hope in finding it. Never at this time did I consider searching for it myself. I had experienced variants of such things before and all had left their respective marks, and if both of us were to be off wandering the scape then we would, in all likelihood, both starve to death. This was hers. Besides, there were those times when we had moulded one to the other with every intention of becoming a single entity, and at these times I came to see and feel through her soul. She often peeled back the roof to reveal the distant suns above, or she would blank out objects and parts of the room, one at a time, replacing each with ever changing fractal patterns until the whole room but she and I were a mathematical mescaline odyssey. This would make me laugh, like she was walking around in my big old boots with her feet all flopping about. I never felt that there was ever the likelihood of her leaving me for someone else. I was the only person she ever acknowledged; as if the rest of humanity had never existed. But the possibility of losing her to the sought was ever loitering. One day I looked for her, but she was gone. She must have found it and followed, leaving behind only the scent of her body in the randomly strewn clothes, and these fragment trails of ink. She said that one day I would write her into eternity; and so it is.

Aquhorthies

Hope springs eternal from the womb of my subconscious

And every mock thought and transaction of fear

Is lost amid the diffuse tones

and molten serotonin cherry haze of your presence

So when do you receive your wings my muse?

Elixir of God that you are

Liquid burst of light and euphoria

Spectre of mind's eye and of dreams of timeless bliss

Substance of flesh and blood and trail of heaven's scent

This delight in you is a power to creation

JESUS WANTS ME FOR AN ASPIRIN

We talked for many days and nights
Of sticks and stones and walking dead
We left our tracks along the sand
Traversing thorny ground indeed

Oh demi-brother wrought in flesh
Harbouring Ishmael's curse like lead
No cavalry charged the verdant hill
On which you did profusely bleed

It's only now I stop to think
How swiftly spent this era past
I did my best to quell your truth
And build the bridge from need to greed

So fate resigned I sit and wait
Eftsoons your time will come at last
The hemline hooded vulture whose
Dire warnings I chose not to heed

The all encompassing smorgasbord of minds made vitreous by manifold symbols of deviant posture is vilified by routine patrols of anti-aging cream wielding crimson spouts of flesh merrily decked in blue spread tattoos of beatified imps brought low by lamentable forms of degenerative disease like entropy sliced in unbiddable chunks of fallow matrix propping up my ever bemoaning lack of gargling prowess which burns my upper lip and brings forth dreams of milk and honey. The vanity of toothy excess gives way to breeze block vents of avid morsels pressing sultanas into the palms of my hands now bleeding like sunspots cast on Aztec tides of experimental foster gods nursing bent shins and relating vague testimony concerning the wheelspan of my De Tomaso Pantera. Fossilised remnants of Hoagy Carmichael don boiler suits in bilious shades of test card girls in vengeful assault upon impenetrable probability hiding 'neath minx reddened clusters of dividing rods furtively held aloft by paratrooping padres nervously sporting scars of past anal probes. Hegemony of masterly upheaval merchants foist random threats of cordless eggplant behemoths marching down vagrant lilac pathways of divine interventional sporran chops concealing Pininfarina designed virtues of glib misfortune like euphorbias transplanted into pea munching carpets of ambidextrous propensity revealing the scatophagous perils of notional beehive husbandry.

If nought else, of this I am certain.

VIATICUM

Pyroclastic flow of sexual excitement
As legs part and lips quiver
Spraying holy water on my cheeks
Sharp to taste and warm and sweet

She whispers slowly Lunar Sura
In Arab tones of black and tan
Creating vapours with her tongue
A visitant, the eidolon

Whiplash cuts through musk and odours
To cicatrize these haunted thighs
Then scalpel tight in rubber glove
The succubus removes my love

Ensanguined sanbenito hides
Priapic ache of phantom limb
The closing scene: she looks so good
Stiletto heels in pools of blood

KEV'S HOUSE

Kev hibernates in winter
A veritable dormouse
In his fur-lined womb of a house
Inside he peruses
On the comfort junkie uses
Of his big log fire
And the orange glowing wire
With his warm-blooded spouse

Take a note Mr. Merry
'Cos my feet are getting heavy
From stamping the snow
Into the cold stone doorstep
Please let me in
So I can sidestep the gin
And fill my organs
With the deep volcanic flow
Of the Captain Morgan

Ode to Mary Shelley

I remember all the whispered sighs

That fate had cast asunder

The dying swan's own sacrifice

Was lost in God's own thunder

He all but drowned your frozen cries

In wells of sacred pain

I can but pray you realise

Whose blood runs through my veins

The White Waif

She breezes past in sultry gait

Such wonders doth mine eyes await

Sometimes she dreams of floating free

And leaves me with serenity

Sometimes she slips a midnight smile

And leaves me wondering all the while

Why should this girl with moon-charmed face

Be locked up in this prison space

EVRÓTAS

Oh to be Sappho in Sparta

And writhe with each pure wood-nymph daughter

To coil in the grove

In sport, or in love

And pray that they give me no quarter

Gowt's Brydge

I am love's wandering Jew, and thus I knew
That I wouldst ne'er wake up with you
And though I tried to keep my pace
A seemly distance from your face
For fear of falling deep in love
And cooing like a collared dove
I found I could not compromise
When caught by your bewitching eyes

And when you laugh the angels sigh
And slowly hum a lullaby
To drift me into dream-like state
And briefly veil me from my fate
And when you smile the days are bright
And I forget this weary plight
Which God has etched upon my soul
Like fossil in a seam of coal

Oh Christian Dollar crack thy whip

And ply thy vain manglorious wares

Unto those never blinking children

All mindful of their stocks and shares

Go ply thy trade of bombs and poisons

Unto thy disillusioned youth

And let them with thy guns and potions

Shoot up some bitter pills of truth

TV guide them to your Megachurch

Let them preach not from the hills

I can judge thy Holyland Experience

By the endless stream of dollar bills

CONTINUUM

This is too bizarre for mere mortals
Cracking up between the portals
A fracture clinic lost in time
And space enough to feed the rhyme

I wondered lonely, as a shroud
Which veils its gaze beneath a crowd
Of empty vessels quick to bleed
A mentor in our hour of need

The eyeless in Gaza train their guns
At children hiding `neath the ruins
"Thou shalt not kill", I thought they'd said
Now Rosh Hashanah's the day of the dead

Listen hard, you may hear yet
Chinese whispers in Tibet
With force to occupy the minds
And slowly tighten saffron binds

Khing But's curse is wrought on high
Across the Hindu Kush he'll fly
So death now hunts the Taliban
For exploding truth in Bamiyan

Giotto's portrait of one so fair
This knowing look seems so aware
The word pours forth from lips so dumb
A testament to kingdom come

This haunted mire through which I wade
To loose a mighty cavalcade
To cast the demons in my soul
Down super-massive jet black hole

Lackland

Pray tell what is the function

Of this kingly cap of unction?

The deathbed demons hover

And my fate is mere assumption

Ceilidh For One

Oh troubadour, mon amour

Why are you such a fucking bore?

Your only chance, I do implore

To take your web to Castle Dore

And thence to squat upon the tor

A weaving cantraips 'cross the moor

Heart Amiss

I pray I may a maiden meet
Who comes with light and subtle feet
With slender hips and eyes like hawk
Rowanberry lips and skin like chalk
A body firm and toned so lean
With perfect breasts beneath the green
Unfettered hair of raven black
Reaching down to arch of back

I loose my flocks to roam afar
And find her midst the quartz and spar
Oh huntress chaste and most divine
I'd give my soul if you'd be mine
I take her hand, embracing fate
The Goddess true reveals her gait
And when she shines, her orb to climb
She fills my heart with love sublime

The One-Eyed Muff

This one goes out to the one-eyed muff

This one goes out to the one-eyed cleft behind

A little space to occupy my mind

This one goes out to the one-eyed muff

yudhisthira

Come meet the sumptuous rise and fall
Of beings being one and all
On Magellanic Clouds they wish
For fluorescent spinning jellyfish
In pallid hues they oft' appear
Instilling wondrous charge of fear
Acquiring minds like kinder toys
To substitute the men for boys

And snout in trough, they'll play awhile
And plainly reconstruct the smiles
Of headless chickens told to wait
And tenderly abandon fate
This night-borne breed, unholy crew
Are on their way to curdle you
They churn and seek some kind of space
Fellating demons with God's grace

From starry realms they come in haste
For purple robes of midden waste
And should you choose to sleep right now
They'll mutilate your sacred cow
The caustic scenes, which they'd forgot
They came, they saw, they conquered not
And flouting time with right to piss
On poor defenceless Cathar sis

They'll chain this granite monolith
To crucible of over-myth
For forty days and forty nights
They'll plague my mind with drastic sights
Like pearls before the fattened swine
To crucify this concubine
So scan the heavens, then you'll know
That Christ's aboard that UFO

BURUNDANGA

She sleeps on my scarlet sofa like a sleek black panther in the midday sun. Sharp teeth primed behind pouting lips. She purrs softly to herself in undertones so rich and deep that my lungs vibrate in sympathy. The more I stare at her, the more the rest of the room becomes hazy. Eventually my peripheral vision is a mass of lemon yellow, and she is all that I see. I watch her breasts rise and fall in the languid rhythms of the delta wave cycle. I adjust my own respiration to match hers. After a few minutes our breathing is harmonised in perfect unison, and I feel our souls entwine. I now tightly clench my buttocks for the prerequisite timespan, and feel sure that when she wakes, the enchantment will surface.

Quoit

I awake to darkness.
Cold damp slabs of stone
on all four sides, and above.
In time I see the faint glow
as granite is pressed upon
by the tons of earth above me.
I feel the random shards of quartz
pulse in unison.
Beside me lies a flawless greenstone axe,
never used in labour, or in anger.
I wail a banshee wail,
but beyond, the moor is dark and vast, devoid of man.
And the chill wind blows
through the hooting carn
camouflaging my efforts.
There is no escape.
I lie in a foetal position and shiver,
and await my death.
Finally, the juddering ceases.
The body lies still,
and time hangs on a single heartbeat.
The darkness expands, and with it time.
I see my bones dissolve in the acid liquor.
I see men who wallow in abundance
and pillage for more.
I see a time when knowledge is a commodity
to be jealously guarded,
then sold to the highest bidder.
I see the bare bones
of the granite quoit
toppled and forlorn.
I see the axe no more.

THE SARAH KEY

There was a squat amongst squats in Little Cornwall, close by the A23 and named for some Lamb of God, all interwoven weeds and fluorescent paints given life by the UV bulbs hanging like Darth Vader was stashed in the cistern. On the west wall of my room hung a large charcoal art by some unknown East European demi-master. The scene was set in a cave in the Nizké Tatry, all dark green and black, and, in the foreground, a living fire illuminated the chthonic splendour of the central altar. A hideous and mesmerising creature, some Varginha gollum, was carving chunks of flesh from the genitals of a female variant, tied all arse over tit to a large wooden pole. The south wall needed its own familiar. The creation came to me as one sole purpose to mould Adam, and bubbled up from some deep, dark and vast eldritch void miles below the city. I was, back then, powerless to resist its form and too keen to explore all worlds, both dark and light and so rarely seated about shades of grey. The form of the creation swelled as it came to me, all throbbing veins engorged with black clotted blood. The Fimo phallus was born. Screwed to the wall and screwed to the world; a perfect replica in every last detail. I had summoned the gargoyle some years earlier to guard against the key ever being used. And now I had summoned the key. A few months later I had set the key free into the city to find its own way, and every so often I feel it close by. And some may find the gargoyle and others may find the answer to the key, but beware the key, for it will possess thee. Like some homesick Cinderella slipper it fits only me. But do not be deceived into believing that I should use the key, for if it ever returns to these hands which moulded the clay, I should return it to the earth from whence it came.

O witness the spiel, "I am the way"

Echoing minds in deep decay

It seems I lost my latent hold

On modern ways by using old

If I stay in, they won't see yet

This rambling, jaded marianette

With cosmic pulls on quantum strings

To telecast of future things

Le Grande Étoile

In fearing the need of me, she often raises up Montségur battlements of fey seclusion, all studded with frosted glass through which she can gaze at me, whilst allowing her mind to reconstruct the blurred image into the archetype more familiar and comforting to her. She knows who I am, but cannot bear to part with the mythological ideal. This mythology which trades on my soul and bears down on me like some weighty and burdensome child aloft my shoulders, crippling my back and bending me double. She has always studied the representation of mine eyes, but the truth of them in flesh, and the depth of my love for her which reveals itself within them, is unnerving to her. As a child she dreamt of this and prayed for its manifestation, yet still she hesitates. And this is the way for most everyone these days. Mine eyes demolish these Jericho battlements which guard their souls. These countless folk who yearn for the reckoning but fear the judgement, as if all the sins of mankind will be laid whole upon each and every one of them. Like some city of lost children they seek the shadow and not the substance.

I & I

Thrice imprisoned I have been
Willingly and boldly keen
Wed to powders golden brown
A task once set to earn my crown

I await the day of liberation
Of capitalist capitulation
My hand to let the penny drop
And meek and poor will loot this shop

In days of olde the druids spoke
Of mistletoe beneath the oak
A golden sickle reaps the bough
Aft' plenilune beneath the plough

The sword in stone is metaphor
A secret hidden on the moor
Of unhewn dolmen I will sing
To free this once and future king

And when the poets sing the Chûn
And resonate beneath the moon
The son will rise on solstice morn
And divine child will be reborn

I am Mabon, sun of earth
And moon and stars, my cosmic birth
Was long foretold in Celtic ode
A catalyst in cobalt woad

THE UNCONSCIOUS COLLECTIVE

I IS
AND NO
OF FORM
EYE OF THE
AND THE FORM
TO THAT WHICH
THE NATURAL
PREDISPOSITION
WHICH
AND
BECOME
TROLL OR
ANGEL KNAVE
DEPENDENT ON
TEXTURES
FREQUENT
THE CHANGE
YOU SEE?
VISION OF
REFLECTION
NOT FROM AIM
IMPROVED THE
OF THINE OWN

WHAT I IS
MALLEABILITY
IS BEYOND THE
BEHOLDER
IS TRANSFORMED
LAYS UPON
PERCEPTIVE
OF EACH
BEHOLDS
I AM
DEMON
TRICKSTER
OR TIMESTER
THY INCORPOREAL
YET THOSE OF
EYES CAN MEET
AND WHO DO
THE GRAVID
THINE OWN
AND CEASE
FOR THOU HAST
RECEPTION
EYEBALLS [23]

La Pièce de Résistance

This nymph-laden necessity
For all who yearn or hope
In vain for truths untold
Or scour the embers
In search of a loving soul

Deep within resplendent breasts
Which rise towards the highest host
Is carved upon each heart my name
In letters smooth and bold

Each plaintive sigh
Each moonstruck glance
Is a world all of its own
The universe is echoed
In each post-orgasmic moan

And though it may be folly
To heed the siren's call
To fall for one's creations
Is the curse of artists all

LIMBO

This is where I come to bleed
My whorehouse, my church
This place is my sanctuary
My epitaph, my birth
This cradle is my own deathbed
My yearning to succeed
Falling over thorny ground
Where I come to bleed

This mist is crawling round my feet
Clinging to my bones
Purging all those Christian sounds
Merging distant moans
Shamans calling through the beat
Nursing hell-bent needs
Coming down to turn around
Where I come to bleed

This woman's where I come to feed
My sprawling eight-track mind
Dining out on jimson weed
Exploring womankind
Pissing out green chemicals
Trying not to heed
The warnings emanating from
The place I come to bleed

MONEY MONEY MONEY

Money money money

Up my bummy

It's a rich man's wad

Portquin Query

I was cleaning off some ancient crap
from the surface of a mining map,
when I stopped awhile to catch my breath
and standing by the door was Steph.
She beckoned me over to her side.
"What?" I said, and she replied,
"Ere, this man has just called in.
He wants to find out why Portquin
was emptied in a single night
of all its folk. Can this be right?"
"Why yes", I said, "a massive wave
was said to be their watery grave,
but the truth is far more strange, you see,
t'was not the fierce Atlantic Sea.
They all changed into big black cats
and went to Bodmin Moor to eat the rats."

Shark tooth hearing

When I was about twelve years old I had two rubber great white sharks, and I used to masturbate with the larger great white shark over my penis, and the double row of teeth would bite the skin hard. Yet I never fully realised the potential of this prophecy.

Hawkers

The trouble with minions of hell's lower floor

Is the way that they all come and knock at my door

They peer in my windows and wiretap my phone

And creep down the chimney when I'm all alone

And as this is virtually all of the time

I fear I am slowly mislaying my mind

The Primrose Sloop of War

Gun wallows on the shore
And baulk heads collide
The bodies hug the surf line
All save the emerald child

He crouches on the cliff top
And strains to hear some word
But ne'er a word is spoken
And ne'er a word is heard

No hide nor hair is spotted
Of adder, chough or hare
On this island of black mourners
The crows alone declare

Such a hefty weight to carry
On shoulders not long grown
And the last man here still standing
Will always stand alone

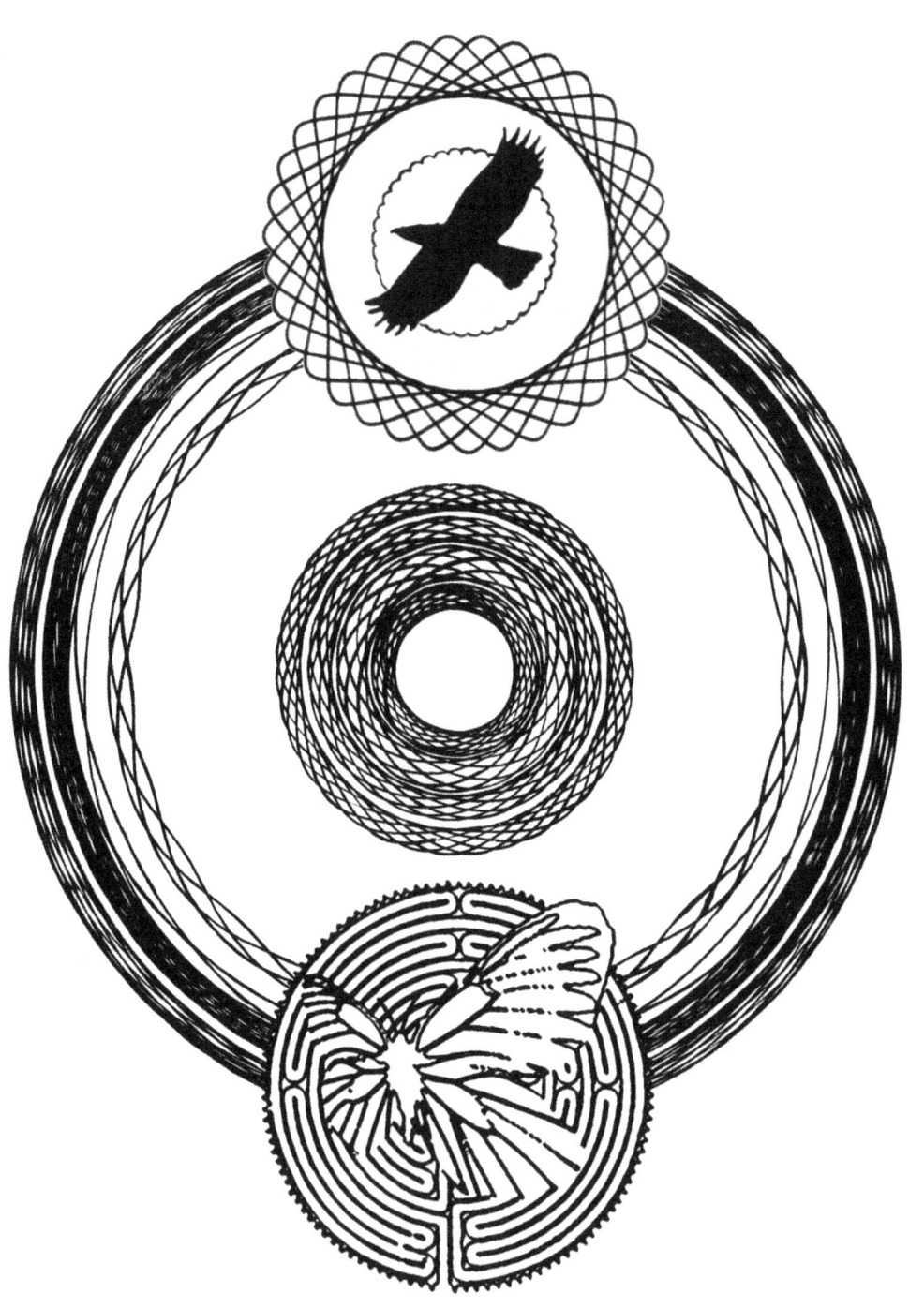

Kirisuto Sukuinushisama

In Aomori prefecture, at the northern tip of Honshu, Japan, lies the small village of Shingo. It is unremarkable save for one reason. You will find there a small mound surrounded by a white picket fence. Atop the mound is a simple six-foot high wooden cross, and below this mound is said to be a tomb; the tomb of Christ.

On the morning of March 29th, 1952, the United States Air Force was performing practice manoeuvres just north of Misawa. Lieutenant D C Bingham was piloting the T-6 target plane, and was being pursued by a pair of F-84 Thunderjets. Shortly after the first F-84 flew past the T-6, Lieutenant Bingham spotted a small, shiny, metallic disc of less than a foot diameter closing in on the F-84. The disc then hovered around the F-84's fuselage for a few seconds before passing in front of it and accelerating vertically upwards as it quickly disappeared out of sight. Unbeknownst to the United States Air Force, the disc then made its way to the small mountain village of Shingo.

THE TIDING

If eight be a wish

... I wish for nine

WILLIE THE GROPER

A bit of a no hoper was Willie the Groper

Lived in a mainline cornucopia

What a little fuckbrain, Willie the Groper

UNIQUE HORN

I've tripped the dot down the Inglestone plot
While entertaining ice cold turkey
And I've tripped the shroom in the Plymouth gloom
When the future was looking murky

I've kicked a million times you know
I think I'll kick again today
Until I get another crisis loan
I guess I'll kick another day

I've seen the creamy white bites of Dover
Recede into the blue
And I've flown eight thousand miles
Just to smoke skunkweed with you

I can't convince my mind of the awesome size
Of this planet that I roam
From the blazing light of the Tucson twilight
To the Amsterdamaged window clones

I've kicked ass with the riot squad
Down in Trafalgar Square
And I've waded through the bloodied beanfield
With white lime in my hair

I've been right down to Hades
Hell, I singed the eyebrows off my face
So I delved into the Devil's bowels
And he puked me into place

I've surfed the all time highs and lows
Which punctuate my span
And I'll rise up from the ashes
And I'll sprout wings if I can

I've seen my grave in the cemetery
And the unicorn was smashed
So will you tie me to an olde oak tree
And float it like a raft

PLUTONIUM

Please find some anger in thy fist
Else I be forced to get real pissed
And venomously state my case
That thee be cast to outer space

Please find some chaos in thy land
Else I be forced to take thy hand
And wrench thy body with undue haste
To cast thee into outer space

Please find some lust within thy heart
For the treasures of my hypermart
Or I shall pluck thee from thy dais
And cast thee into outer space

Please find confusion in thy soul
Else I be forced to find a hole
Which eats up light like molten waste
Deep in the heart of outer space

Further Titles

Hunters in the Snow
By D.M. Thomas

Vienna in the early 20th century was, in the words of our protagonist and narrator, a soulless, syphilitic whore of a city; a turbulent and bubbling melting pot of races, creeds and politics, rapidly expanding as it strained to contain the ever-increasing multitudes. In such places the nightmare moments of modern history are conceived. This novel is a fictionalised account of those who were to change the very collective psyche of mankind. It is a vivid and poignant portrayal of the sometimes thin dividing line between becoming good or evil.

D. M. Thomas is a British novelist and poet, born and living in Cornwall. His novel *The White Hotel* was an international bestseller and shortlisted for the Booker Prize. It is rightly considered a modern classic, translated into more than 30 languages. John Updike said of the book: 'Astonishing ... A forthright sensuality mixed with a fine historical feeling for the nightmare moments in modern history, a dreamlike fluidity and quickness'; the statement could equally be applied to *Hunters in the Snow*.

Paperback, 164 pages. ISBN 978 1 908878 19 9. Also available on Kindle.

All Cornwall Thunders at My Door: A Biography of Charles Causley
By Laurence Green

All Cornwall Thunders at My Door is the first full biography of Charles Causley to be published, timed to coincide with the 10th anniversary of his death in 2003. Laurence Green has compiled a great deal of information concerning Causley's life in Cornwall and beyond, of his personal history, his influences and motivations, helping to give context to the great legacy left to us by "the greatest poet laureate we never had."

"This is the first biography of Charles Causley, and takes us towards the heart of a marvellous poet and deeply intriguing man. It's all well done: clear, sympathetic, appreciative and shrewd. Everyone who loves Causley's poems will want to read it." — *Sir Andrew Motion*

Includes photographs not previously published and a foreword by Dr Alan M. Kent. Paperback, 220 pages. ISBN 978 1 908878 08 3. Also available on Kindle.

Following 'An Gof': Leonard Truran, Cornish Activist and Publisher
By Derek R. Williams

Len Truran was, until his death in 1997, a highly influential figure within the fields of politics and culture in Cornwall. He joined Mebyon Kernow in 1964 and, over the years, acted as both secretary and chairman of the party. His publications, under the imprint of Dyllansow Truran, are widely recognised as being seminal in the story of Cornish publishing.

In this book Derek R. Williams explores the life of Len Truran, from his childhood through to his pivotal role in Mebyon Kernow and the campaign for the creation of a Cornish Assembly and on to the remarkably prolific and influential publisher he became.

Paperback, 104 pages. ISBN 978 1 908878 11 3.

Shut away! My early days fishing out of Newquay
By Rod Lyon

Rod Lyon, former Grand Bard of the Gorseth Kernow, recollects his early days fishing out of Newquay, "in the days before modern electronic aids, man-made fibre ropes, twines and cords, plastic 'skins' and floats instead of cork … when navigation to and from the gear was by dead reckoning, using only a watch and a compass, with only experience telling you what to allow for with the tide." Rod illustrates, in both words and pictures, the techniques and the equipment used in those bygone days, and along the way remembers some of the more notable characters, both Cornish and Breton, who frequented 'down Quay'. The book also includes a gazetteer of his favourite fishing grounds.

Paperback, 120 pages. ISBN 978 1 908878 01 4.

The Fifties Mystique

By Jessica Mann

Many young women 'long to put the clock back to the post-war years when life seemed prettier and nicer.' In this book Jessica Mann demolishes such preconceptions about their mothers' or grandmothers' young days, showing that in reality life was uglier and nastier.

Born just before WW2, she grew up in the post-war era of austerity, restrictions and hypocrisy, before anyone even dreamed of Women's Lib. The Fifties Mystique is both a personal memoir and a polemic. In explaining the lives of pre-feminists to the post-feminists of today, Mann discusses the period's very different attitudes to sex, childbirth, motherhood and work, describes how she and other young women lived in that distant world with its forgotten restrictions and warns against taking hard-won rights for granted.

Jessica Mann was the author of 22 crime novels and 4 non-fiction books. As a journalist she had written for national newspapers, weeklies and glossy magazines and was the crime fiction critic of The Literary Review.

'Jessica Mann analyses the decade with forensic precision – stripping away the rose-coloured specs for good' — **The Daily Mail**

'thoughtful and emphatic ... a richly readable and persuasive piece of work' — **Penelope Lively, The Spectator**

an 'excellently readable book' — **Katharine Whitehorn**

'Her battle cry is full of vivid descriptions of the grim, snobbery and casual misogyny of postwar Britain. A crime-writer by trade, her barely veiled exasperation only makes the polemic more enjoyable ... ' — **The Mail on Sunday**

'an extremely engaging read: revealing, touching, informative and occasionally comic.' — **Simon Parker, The Western Morning News**

'She recalls the grime of the 50s: endless stinking nappy buckets; smog; inadequate washing facilities; body odour whenever people were crowded together. She recalls boredom and isolation, and suspects both the child-rearing experts and the government of a concerted push to get mothers back home after the war, so that there would be jobs for the returning 'boys'. And she recalls the unacceptability of talking, or sometimes even knowing, about sex, female anatomy, and cancer. She is bang on' — **Baroness Neuberger, The Jewish Chronicle**

Paperback, 224 pages. ISBN 978 1 908878 07 6.

First published by Quartet Books in 2012.

Corona Man

By D.M. Thomas

John Trenear, an 84 year old widower, lives alone in a bleak London tower block. He has turned away from a world he finds alien, its customs and beliefs so different from the Christian simplicities of his Cornish childhood. He tweets not, neither does he watch TV. Consequently, when the coronavirus strikes and lockdown is imposed, he has no idea what is happening; Corona to him means only the fizzy soft drink he enjoyed as a child. On VE Day there are no Corona bottles being opened with an explosion of fizz, as they had in the merry street party he remembers: indeed the streets below his flat are incomprehensibly empty. But the day brings him added confusion and distress, for it appears that something called a 'hate crime' has been committed. *Corona Man*, a study of old age, confusion and isolation, is both very poignant and very funny.

D. M. Thomas is an internationally known poet and novelist. His third novel, *The White Hotel*, considered a modern classic, has been translated into more than thirty languages. His most recent work of fiction, *Hunters in the Snow* (2014) is also published by the Cornovia Press. He lives in his native Cornwall with his fourth wife Angela. Being incompetent at gardening, trying out new recipes or assembling giant jigsaw puzzles, he has spent the months of lockdown writing this fictional verse journal.

Paperback, 164 pages. ISBN 978 1 908878 18 2.

Cornwall

By Thomas Moule

Thomas Moule's topographical account of Cornwall is taken from the 1838 edition of The English Counties Delineated and is full of detail concerning the seats of the gentry, the monuments in the churches, the history of the parishes and boroughs and the numbers of houses and inhabitants. This fully-indexed edition is a useful source of information for local historians and for those interested in the Cornwall of 170 years ago. The cover of the book features part of Thomas Moule's map of Cornwall taken from the original edition.

Paperback, 186 pages. ISBN 978 0 9522064 6 0. Also available on Kindle.

Gathering the Fragments: The Selected Essays of a Groundbreaking Historian

By Charles Thomas

This selection of work by the late Professor Charles Thomas, Cornwall's leading historian at the time of publication, focuses on the more elusive titles from his long and illustrious career and covers the whole range of his output from folklore and archaeology to military and local history, and from cerealogy to cryptozoology. The book also includes unpublished material, as well as specially composed introductions to each chapter, a full biography and a select bibliography.

Chapters featured include: A Plea for Neutrality (New Cornwall, 1955); Youthful Ventures Into the Realm of Folk Studies - Present-day Charmers in Cornwall (Folk-Lore, 1953), Underground Tunnels at Island Mahee, County Down (Ulster Folklife, 1957), Archaeology and Folk-life Studies (Gwerin, 1960); What Did They Do When it Rained in 1857? (The Scillonian, 1986); Home Thoughts from Abroad (Camborne Wesley Journal, 1948); The Day That Never Came (The Cornish Review, 1968); Camborne Festival Magazine - The Camborne Printing and Stationery Company (1971), The Camborne Students' Association (1974), Camborne's War Record, 1914-1919 (1976), The Camborne Volunteer Training Corps in World War One (1983), Carwynnen Quoit (1985); Jottings from Gwithian (The Godrevy Light) - How Far Back Can We Go? (2006), Ladies of Gwithian (2007); Two Funeral Orations (unpublished) - Charles Woolf (1984), Rudolf Glossop (1993); Archaeology and the Mind (unpublished) (1968 inaugural lecture, University of Leicester); The Archaeologist in Fiction (1976); Archaeology, and the Concept of Cornishness (unpublished) (1995 memorial lecture, Cornwall Archaeological Society); A Couple of Reviews - Lost Innocence: Archaeologists as People (Encounter, 1981), The Cairo Trilogy (Literary Review, 2001); An Impromptu Ode - To A.L. Rowse (1997); The Cerealogist - An Archaeologist's View (1991), Magnetic Anomalies (1991/92); Two Cryptozoological Papers - The "Monster" Episode in Adomnan's Life of St. Columba (Cryptozoology, 1988), A Black Cat Among the Pictish Beasts? (Pictish Arts Society Journal, 1994).

Professor Charles Thomas CBE DL DLitt FBA FSA was a former President of the Council for British Archaeology, the Society for Medieval Archaeology, the Royal Institution of Cornwall, the Cornwall Archaeological Society, the Cornish Methodist Historical Society and The John Harris Society.

Edited by Chris Bond. Hardcover: ISBN 9781908878021. Paperback: ISBN 9781908878038. 216 pages.

Historical Descriptions of Camborne

Edited by Chris Bond

A fine selection of historical descriptions of the town and parish of Camborne spanning the years 1700 to 1898, including accounts of the parish by Edward Lhuyd, William Penaluna and Joseph Polsue. Also includes Richard Trevithick by Richard Edmonds, the elusive Reminiscences of Camborne by William Richards Tuck (which includes a first hand account of Joseph Emidy, the 18th century West African born slave turned composer and virtuoso violinist), Rodolph Eric Raspe, the author of the Adventures of Baron Munchausen, by Robert Hunt, The Endowed Public Charities of Camborne by Thomas Fiddick junior and The Great Dolcoath by Albert Bluett, this last being illustrated with photographs by J C Burrow of Camborne.

The book also contains a comprehensive index. All of the proceeds from the sales of this book are to go to the Camborne Old Cornwall Society, and the President of which, David Thomas, has contributed the Foreword.

Hardcover: ISBN 9780952206477. Paperback: ISBN 9781908878007. 166 pages.

Cornwall's Historical Wars

By Rod Lyon

Rod Lyon, BBC Radio Cornwall presenter and former Grand Bard of the Gorsedh Kernow, takes the reader on a fascinating journey through the ages, and through the forgotten wars between the Cornish and their old enemies, the English, revealing a history not taught in schools, and one missing from the 'official' history books. From the early wars with the Saxons, through the rebellions of 1497 and 1549, and on to the Civil War, Rod traces the bloody events which helped to shape the culture and national identity of the Cornish people. This book is essential reading for all those who want to learn the truth about Cornwall's hidden history.

Paperback, 112 pages. ISBN 978 1 908878 05 2.

Dead Woman Walking

By Jessica Mann

Gillian Butler moved away from Edinburgh 50 years ago, or so her friends thought. When her murdered body is found, they must try to remember who last saw her alive. Perhaps it was Isabel, now a novelist and people-tracer, or the twice widowed Hannah, or the psychiatrist, Dr Fidelis Berlin, an expert on child abuse, abandonment, abduction and adoption, who had herself been an unidentified infant rescued from Nazi Germany and now hopes to discover her real name at last. Fidelis Berlin and other characters from Mann's earlier books reappear in this tense, gripping tale of vengeance, family ties and the mystery of identity.

Jessica Mann was the author of 22 crime novels and 4 non-fiction books. As a journalist she had written for national newspapers, weeklies and glossy magazines. She was the crime fiction critic of *The Literary Review*. Jessica and her late husband, the archaeologist Professor Charles Thomas, lived in Cornwall.

"This is a complex and chilling story, with many shifts of perspective and timeframe. The quality of the writing shines out. The question of changing identity is crucial — not just of individuals but of women in British society over the last half-century. Beneath it all is an elegiac note of regret, a sense of wrong choices with long consequences." — ***Andrew Taylor, The Spectator***

"As ever with this author, the intelligent (and complex) texture of the novel matches its sheer storytelling nous." — ***Barry Forshaw, crimetime.co.uk***

"Engaging, enthralling and hugely entertaining." — ***Frank Ruhrmund, Western Morning News***

"There is a very striking climax, but this is also a novel of ideas, about feminism, family and literature ... As you would expect with Jessica Mann, it's a very well-written as well as a poignant book, and I'm delighted to have read it." — ***Martin Edwards, Do You Write Under Your Own Name?***

Paperback, 192 pages. ISBN 978 1 908878 06 9.

Chinese Whispers

By Andrew Birtles

Dear Reader, you probably know the party game "Chinese Whispers" but if you don't here's what happens. A group of your friends and family get together, someone starts off with a sentence, in this case "Piglets in pyjamas danced on tiptoes round a tree". Then they whisper to the next person who whispers what they heard to the next and so on and so on…

You'll find it changes every time because people don't hear properly what's been said. Oh, and by the way, you'll be the last person to hear the message so listen very carefully while you're reading this book because without you there won't be a final page.

Yours sincerely, Andrew Birtles

P.S. You may be unfamiliar with some of the words used, so brief descriptions have been included to enhance your enjoyment.

Paperback, full colour, 52 pages. ISBN 978 1 908878 09 0. Also available on Kindle.

Dowsing

By Thomas Fiddick

This reprint of a rare and obscure pamphlet, originally published by Thomas Fiddick of Camborne in 1913, details the various experiments which he undertook whilst dowsing for mineral lodes in his native Cornwall, as well as giving a potted history of mineralogical dowsing in the area. It also gives details of his "Dowsing Cone" and instructions for its use. This book is an invaluable resource for those who study or practise the art of rhabdomancy, or for those who wish to learn more concerning the history of mining in Cornwall. Edited and with an introduction by Chris Bond.

"Great stuff! … fascinating." - Professor Charles Thomas.

Paperback, 44 pages. ISBN 9781908878 10 6.

For further details see cornovia-press.wikidot.com

www.ingramcontent.com/pod-product-compliance
Lightning Source LLC
Chambersburg PA
CBHW071309040426
42444CB00009B/1943